Maple Sugaring at Home

Joe McHale

Reine Publishing Group, LLC

© 2010, 2013 by Joe McHale

Second Edition with Revisions, 2013

Cover design by Neil Secretario, Oceanfront Studio

ISBN 978-0-9831256-0-0

Published by Reine Publishing Group, LLC

Contact us at info@reinepublishing.com

Printed in the United States of America

Table of Contents

Introduction

I started tapping maple trees as an exciting way to teach my children about nature and the origin of food. Inspired by my own search for information, this fun activity led to the creation of Tap My Trees and to the writing of this guide. The goal of Tap My Trees is to promote the tapping of maple trees by families at home as well as to provide the essential equipment and information to get started. This guide outlines the step-by-step instructions for backyard sugaring and should serve as a friendly and informative guide as to the process.

Tapping trees provides hours of enjoyment and a worthwhile educational experience. This engaging and environmentally friendly event will be gratifying for those of all ages, from school children to grandparents. Once collected, the sap may be utilized as a nutritional drink, a liquid substitute in recipes and, of course, boiled down into maple syrup.

Take a walk with me through each step of the maple sugaring process, from equipment needed, to identifying your maple trees, to boiling your sap into syrup. My hope is that this information will inspire and encourage you to tap your maple trees and to make syrup in the comfort of your own home. Please consider this a wonderful opportunity for families to "tap" into nature and, in doing so, create lasting memories of this fun-filled family activity.

Happy Tapping!

Joe McHale

Equipment

Maple sugaring equipment is quite simple. First and foremost, one needs a maple tree! A spile, hook, and bucket are the other essential supplies necessary to get started. While more ambitious sap collectors may utilize tubing collection systems, the beginner can use a bucket or even a clean, plastic jug. When it comes time to boil your sap, a simple fire source will suffice. As you expand your operation, you may choose to seek out an evaporator, but it is definitely not required in small scale productions.

While the focus here will be on the use of traditional supplies, feel free to experiment and utilize materials you already own to get started. For example, instead of a bucket, you may choose to use clean milk gallon jugs. Use your imagination! Have fun with it and enjoy the simplicity of the process.

Maple Tree: Let's start with the obvious. You will need a maple tree! That is to say, you will need a healthy, mature maple tree at least twelve inches in diameter.

A tree with a twelve inch diameter will be able to sustain one tap. When

it is time for your first tapping, it is suggested that you tap three trees. Assuming each tree is tapped once and all the sap collected is boiled into syrup, each tree should produce approximately one quart of maple syrup. Need help identifying your maple trees? Refer to the next section of this guide.

Spile: Also known as a tap or spout, the spile is used to transfer the maple sap from the tree into a bucket. Spiles are generally made from stainless steel, aluminum, or plastic.

Hook: A hook is either provided with the spile or is incorporated into the design of the spile.

Bucket: A bucket is used to collect maple sap as it drips from the spile. Buckets come in a variety of sizes, from two gallon to four gallon, and can be made from plastic, steel, or aluminum. The benefits of plastic buckets are that they are less expensive and will not dent with years of use. While metal buckets are more expensive, they provide a more nostalgic image. You may be able to obtain used metal buckets, but buyer beware as they may leak or be corroded. Use buckets specifically designed for collecting maple sap or use other food grade containers. Caution: metal buckets designed for other purposes may leach lead or zinc into the sap. An economical alternative to buckets is to use a plastic milk jug. Simply attach the jug to the spile with wire.

Lid: The lid plays an important role. It prevents rain, snow, and foreign material from entering the bucket. Lids are generally made from plastic, galvanized metal, or stainless steel. The lid does not form a tight seal on the bucket, but is hung from the spile over the bucket to allow easy bucket retrieval when collecting the sap. Note that some lids are designed to clip onto the top of the bucket.

Drill Bit and Drill: To make the necessary hole in the tree, a drill and drill bit are needed. Most spiles require a 7/16 inch drill bit. There are some varieties of spiles that utilize a 5/16 inch drill bit. It is suggested to use a cordless drill as you will most likely be tapping trees that are not near an electrical source. **Do not use an extension cord across wet or snow covered ground.**

Storage Containers: After collecting your sap, you will need a place to store it prior to boiling it down into maple syrup. Clean plastic milk jugs, juice bottles or food grade five gallon buckets may be used. It is extremely important to carefully clean all containers that were previously used as any residue could give your syrup an off taste or even spoil your hard work. Assuming you tap three trees and boil your sap once a week, you should plan on storing approximately fifteen gallons of sap.

Cheesecloth: Your collected sap may contain pieces of bark, a thirsty moth, or other foreign materials. Use cheesecloth to filter any solids when transferring sap from the collection bucket to a storage container.

Hammer: A hammer is used to gently tap the spile into the tap hole.

Pliers: Pliers are used to remove the tap from the tree once the maple sugaring season is over.

Sap Processing Equipment: The number one use of maple sap is to

make maple syrup. To boil sap into syrup, the hobbyist at home can use anything from pots and pans on an outdoor fire pit to a professional evaporator. The Section "Making Maple Syrup" will provide more details and options to boil sap into maple syrup. Pictured is a homemade evaporator utilizing a 55 gallon drum.

Identifying Maple Trees

Have you ever gazed into your yard and wondered, "What types of trees are here?" "What kinds of trees may be tapped?" "Are any of my trees suitable for tapping?" If so...you are not alone.

The ideal time of year to identify maple trees is in the summer or fall. This is because the leaves are still on the tree and the leaf is the easiest way to identify a tree. During the summer or fall draw a map of your yard. Plot the location of each maple tree. Be sure to include the type of each maple. The dilemma comes during the winter when you have no such map. Without leaves on the trees it is difficult to identify which trees are maple. In this case, you have some options:

- Look at the bark and compare it to the descriptions found later in this section for each type of maple tree.
- Look for the fruit of the maple tree on the nearby ground. The fruit is the "helicopter" that you threw in the air as a child and watched as it spiraled downward to the ground.
- Do you remember the bright red tree during the fall? There's a good chance that it was a Red Maple tree.
- If you are feeling confident, twig and bud identification is another way to tell which kind of trees you have.

In any case, prepare that map of your trees for next season. On the next page is an example of a yard map.

Example of a Yard Map

Due to their sugar content, the following trees are most commonly tapped for sap collection:

- Sugar Maple
- Black Maple
- Red Maple
- Silver Maple

These maples are listed in order of tapping preference, as the Sugar Maple sap will have the highest sugar content, the Black Maple sap will have the next highest sugar content, and so forth. This is not to say that other types of maples cannot be tapped, such as the Box-elder (also known as the Ash-leaved Maple) but the resulting sap will have a lower sugar content.

There is a direct correlation between sugar content in sap and the amount of boiling time required to convert this sap into maple syrup. The higher the sugar content, the less boiling time required.

Sugar Maple sap will have an average sugar content of 2-2.5%, requiring approximately forty gallons of sap to produce one gallon of syrup. The sugar content of other types of maple trees listed will vary between 1% and 1.5%. This will require a greater quantity of sap and a longer boiling time to generate the same one gallon of syrup. Also note that a tree's sugar content varies season to season and will also change throughout the sugaring season with the highest sugar content at the beginning of the season.

While this guide focuses on maple trees, other varieties of trees can be tapped. For example, Birch and Walnut trees may be tapped and will yield a sweet sap. These trees are not generally used in commercial production of syrup because the sugar content is lower. In Alaska, where maple trees do not grow, there is a thriving Birch sap industry. In Eastern Europe, the Birch tree is used to collect "birch juice". Ukrainians and Russians drink this juice as a way to ingest the essence of nature each spring.

In addition to leaf shape, the distinctive fruit can also be used to identify maple trees. Fertilized female flowers develop into samaras, with seeds attached to flattened wings. A good wind can carry the samara 100 yards. Feeding birds, squirrels, chipmunks, and mice also distribute the 50,000 to 100,000 seeds produced by a mature maple tree each year. Generally only one of the paired samaras contains a viable seed.

Maple trees are at risk to the Asian Longhorned Beetle, a beetle native to China that is causing widespread destruction of trees in the United States and Canada. The larvae bore into the trees heartwood to feed on the tree's nutrients. This eventually kills the tree. Eradication efforts require the tree to be cut down, chipped, and burned. Often thousands of trees are removed and destroyed when an infestation is found. Signs of infestation include perfectly round 1 cm holes, oozing sap, and sawdust on or around the tree. If you suspect an Asian Longhorned Beetle infestation, contact your local forestry officials.

Sugar Maple (Acer saccharum) Characteristics

The high sugar content of the Sugar Maple's sap makes it ideal for tapping. Large scale maple sugaring operations rely on these trees, often grown in a large grove known as a sugar bush. The presence of the Sugar Maple leaf on the Canadian flag illustrates the importance of this tree in Canada. The Sugar Maple grows to approximately 100 feet tall with a trunk diameter of 3 to 4 feet. The wood is hard and close grained; therefore, it is used in applications requiring strength such as bowling lanes, baseball bats, and cutting blocks.

Habitat: Within the United States, the Sugar Maple is found in the northeast, extending south to Tennessee. Within Canada, it can be found in southern Ontario and Quebec.

Sugar Maple habitat within the United States.

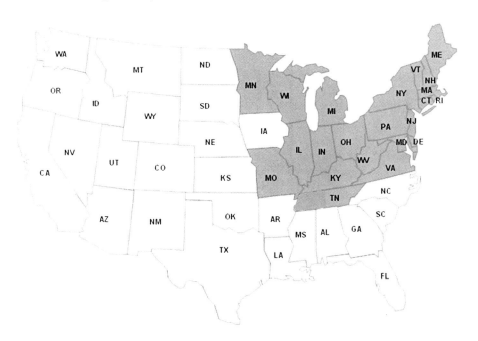

Leaf: The Sugar Maple leaf is rounded at the base, extending to generally 5 lobes. The tips of the lobes are pointed, but the edges are smooth (without fine teeth compared to Red and Silver Maples). The leaf is approximately 3-5 inches long and slightly more across. There is a slight "U" shape where the stem meets the leaf. The texture is thin but firm, with a bright green color and a paler green underside.

Bark: The bark on young trees is dark grey and smooth. On mature trees, the bark is dark brown and develops vertical grooves and ridges that vary from light grey to dark brown.

Twig / Bud: The twig is somewhat shiny reddish-brown, and slender. This smooth twig generates a bud 1/4 to 3/8 inch long, conical, pointed, and brown in color.

Note that all maples mentioned in this section will have opposite paired arrangement of its buds/leaves and twig, meaning they are aligned on opposite sides of the branch. Illustrated is an example of an opposite paired arrangement.

Fruit: The fruit looks like the helicopter-winged seed you threw into the air as a child and then watched as it spiral to the ground. The seeds join each other in a straight line, while the wings are separated by approximately 60 degrees. Each winged seed is about 1 inch long. The fruit ripens in early fall and begins dropping before the leaves fall. Some fruit may persist on the tree into the winter.

Black Maple (Acer nigrum) Characteristics

The Black Maple resembles the Sugar Maple and is often considered in the same family as the Sugar Maple. The most significant difference is the 3-lobed leaf of the Black Maple versus the 5-lobed leaf of the Sugar Maple. The Black Maple grows to approximately 100 feet tall. Fall color ranges from bright yellow, orange, or a red-orange. It has a life span of over 200 years.

Habitat: Within the United States, the Black Maple is found in the mid north-eastern states, from southern Wisconsin to northern Tennessee. Within Canada, it is found in the extreme southern portions of Ontario and Quebec.

Black Maple habitat within the United States.

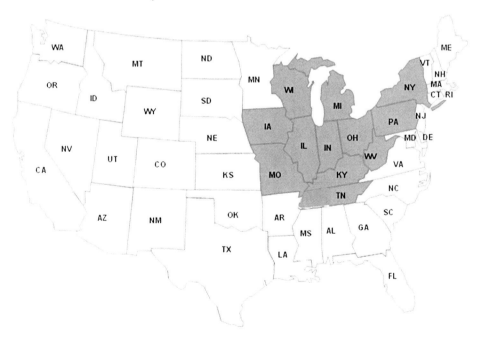

Leaf: Similar to the Sugar Maple, but has 3 lobes instead of 5. On the tree, the leaf often appears to be drooping.

Bark: The bark is similar to the Sugar Maple, but a bit darker and with deeper grooves.

Twig / Bud: The twig is somewhat shiny, brown, and slender, with small warty growths. Older twigs will have a waxy coating. Buds are conical, pointed, brown in color, and often hairy.

Fruit: Similar to the Sugar Maple, with a slightly larger seed. The fruit matures in the fall.

Red Maple (Acer rubrum) Characteristics

The Red Maple is named to reflect its brilliant red autumn foliage. Due to its ability to thrive in a wide variety of soils and climates, the Red Maple is one of the most common hardwood trees in North America. The Red Maple reaches a height of 60 - 90 feet; it has the ability to grow in both dry and wet soil conditions and enjoys a life span up to 150 years.

Habitat: Within the United States, the Red Maple is found in all eastern states, and as far west as Minnesota and Arkansas. Within Canada, it is found in southern Ontario and Quebec.

Red Maple habitat within the United States.

Leaf: The leaf is 2 - 6 inches wide, usually with 3 lobes. The margins of the leaf contain small, sharp teeth. The mature leaves are light green with a whitish underside. In the fall they turn to a deep red color. On a twig, leaves develop directly across from their opposites.

Bark: The bark on young trees is light grey and smooth. On mature trees, the bark is darker, with grey or black ridges and narrow, scaly plates.

Twig / Bud: The twig is slender, shiny, and reddish in color. Buds are blunt, clustered, and 1/8—1/4 inch long.

Fruit: The V-shaped, double-winged fruit develops in clusters, and is ½ - 1 inch long. The fruit matures in the spring (as opposed to the fall for a Sugar or Black Maple). The color is initially bright red, but turns brown before it drops from the tree.

Silver Maple (Acer saccharinum) Characteristics

The Silver Maple is a rapidly growing tree and, like the Red Maple, is able to thrive in a wide variety of soils and climates. When the twig is scraped or broken, a strong foul odor is detected. The Silver Maple reaches a height of between 70 - 100 feet tall. The Silver Maple trunk often splits into multiple vertical limbs low in the tree. This tree has brittle wood and is commonly damaged in storms. The wood is soft and not used where strength is required.

Habitat: Within the United States, the Silver Maple is found in the eastern states, south to Georgia and west to Nebraska. Within Canada, it is found only in the extreme southern portions of Ontario and Quebec.

Silver Maple habitat within the United States.

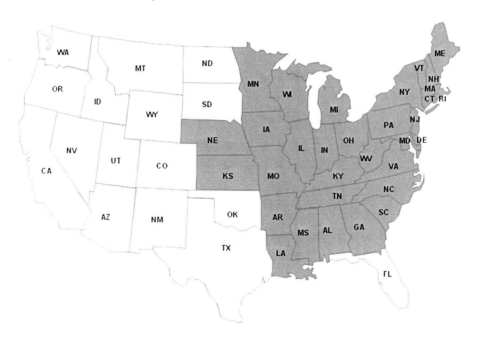

Leaf: The leaf is 5 - 7 inches wide with 5 lobes. The margins of the leaf contain fine teeth. The mature leaves are pale green with a silvery white underside (hence the name Silver Maple).

Bark: The bark on young trees is grey with a reddish tint. On mature trees, the long thin scaly plates produce a shaggy appearance. The color is reddish brown.

Twig / Bud: The twig and bud are similar to the Red Maple. When the twig is broken, a foul smell is detected. Winter buds are slightly larger than those on the Red Maple.

Fruit: The double-winged fruit develops in clusters and is 1 ½ - 2 inches long. Often one of the seeds is underdeveloped. The fruit matures in the spring.

Tapping Trees

Congratulations! At this point, you have gathered your equipment and have identified your maple trees. You are now ready to tap your trees. Let the fun begin!

When to Tap: Maple sap generally begins to flow between early-February and March. The exact time of year depends upon where you live and weather conditions, and could start as early as January. Sap flows when daytime temperatures rise above freezing (32 degrees Fahrenheit / 0 Celsius) and nighttime temperatures fall below freezing. Ideal conditions are low-40's (Fahrenheit) during the day and mid-20's (Fahrenheit) during the night. The rising temperature creates pressure in the tree thereby generating the flow of sap. This is basically a transfer of the sap from the tree above the ground and the root system below the ground. Generally the sap flows for 4 to 6 weeks, with the best sap produced early in the sap-flowing season. The end of the season occurs when the temperature remains above freezing or buds begin to mature on the tree. The sap will also take on a yellow or milky color and have an off taste known as "buddy sap".

Collect and Clean the Supplies:

- Spiles / Hooks
- Buckets / Lids
- Drill Bit
- Drill
- Hammer

Clean spiles, buckets, and lids prior to use each season. Using a mixture of 1 part unscented household bleach (such as Clorox® Regular-Bleach) to 20 parts clean water, use a brush or cloth to scrub your supplies. Triple rinse all with hot water.

Trees: Using the information in the "Identify Maple Trees" section, you should have already identified your maple trees. The first choice for tapping is Sugar and Black Maples and the second choice is Red and Silver Maples. Select trees to tap that are mature (at least 12 inches in diameter) and healthy. The tree on the edge of your driveway that is healing from a direct car hit is not an ideal candidate for tapping! If you have many maple trees to choose from, select trees with open southern exposure and an abundance of branches. If you have a limited number of maples available, you can tap a particular tree two or three times, depending upon its size. A healthy tree will support multiple taps, but use the following guidelines:

Tree Diameter	Number of Taps
12 - 20 inches	1
21 - 27 inches	2
Greater than 27 inches	3

Where to Tap: The height of the tap hole does not have an impact on sap collection. The tap location should be at a height that is convenient for you and allows easy collection, generally at a height of about 3 feet. Be sure to take into consideration any accumulation of snow on the ground, or your buckets may be too high on the tree for easy retrieval when the snow melts. If the tree has been tapped in previous seasons, do not tap within 4 inches to the side of and 6 inches above or below a previous tap hole. Ideally, the tap hole should be above a large root or below a large branch on the south side of the tree. If more than one tap is to be placed in the same tree, distribute the tap holes around the circumference of the tree. Always be sure to avoid any damaged area of the tree.

Drilling the Tap Hole: Using a 7/16 inch drill bit, drill a hole 2 to 2 ½ inches deep. It may be helpful to wrap a piece of tape around the drill bit 2 ½ inches from the tip to use as a depth guide. Drill at a slight upward angle to facilitate downward flow of sap from the hole. To help pull the

shavings out and ensure a clean hole, keep the drill bit rotating as you pull the bit out of the tree. A helpful hint in getting all the shavings out is to use a small twig to help pull them from the tap hole. The shavings from the drilled tap hole should be light brown, indicating healthy

sapwood. If the shavings are dark brown, this indicates you have drilled into a damaged portion of the tree. You should drill another hole in a different location. A cordless drill is recommended, but a corded electric drill can be used with a properly insulated extension cord long enough to reach the tree.

Inserting the Spile: Clear any wood shavings away from the edge of the hole. Insert the spile into the loop on the hook (hook facing outward), and then insert the spile into the tap hole. Gently tap the spile into the tree with a hammer. Do not aggressively pound the spile into the tree especially if the tree is frozen because this may cause the bark to split. If the bark splits it may be difficult to properly seat the tap into the tree, causing leakage and slowing down the healing process once the season is done. If the spile is not seated correctly you may notice a wet stain on the tree, this is the tree's way of publicly announcing a poor tapping job! Do not pull the spile out if this happens; just reseat the spile by gently tapping it until it is firmly set into the tree. If the sap is flowing, it will immediately start dripping from the spile.

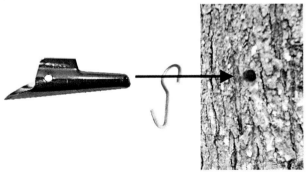

Hanging the Bucket: Hang the bucket by inserting the hook into the hole on the rim of the bucket. Both metal and plastic buckets are hung in the same manner. If you are using a one gallon plastic jug to collect your sap, cut a one inch round hole in the stem of the jug and use a wire to secure the jug to the spile.

Attaching the Lid: Attach the lid to the spile by inserting the metal wire through the double holes on the spile. The function of the lid is to keep out snow, rain, and foreign materials. Both the metal and plastic lid attach to the spile in the same manner. If using a plastic milk jug, keep the round lid attached to the top of the jug. Note that some metal buckets have a different style lid that clips onto the top of the bucket. This style is not illustrated here.

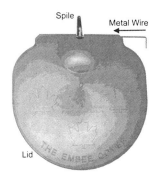

Congratulations, you have successfully tapped your maple tree!

Collecting and Storing Sap

You have successfully tapped your trees and now the sap is flowing faster than you can boil it; what to do with all the sap?

Depending upon the weather conditions, sap will begin to flow immediately after inserting the tap. You will be able to watch it drip from the tap into the bucket. Maple sap is a clear fluid similar in look to water. It's a little sweet too, taste it!

Although the collection amount will vary, you can expect to collect 5 to 15 gallons of sap per tap per season. Do not be discouraged if some days you only collect a small amount of sap as other days your buckets will surely overflow. In addition, each tap is a little different, so some will produce more sap than others. Two taps holes on the same tree will likely produce different amounts of sap.

Storage Containers: Sap is generally not boiled daily therefore storage containers are used to store the sap until you are ready to boil. Use only food grade containers to store your collected sap. Clean plastic milk jugs or juice containers may be used. You can also use 5 gallon buckets (food grade quality). Your local deli or donut shop may provide these free of charge as they often receive their ingredients in such containers. Be sure all containers are thoroughly cleaned using a mixture of one part unscented household bleach (such as Clorox® Regular-Bleach) to 20 parts clean water. Scrub the containers and triple rinse with hot water.

Transfer from Bucket to Storage Container: When sap is flowing, collect it daily. Pour the sap from the bucket into the storage container using cheesecloth to filter out any foreign material. If the top layer of the sap has frozen, this frozen portion can be thrown away (Note: it is difficult to break down this ice if you are transferring the sap to a container with

a neck). While the ice may have some sugar content in it, the ice in a partially frozen bucket will have a much lower sugar content than the liquid sap. Discarding the ice will actually help when it comes time to boil your sap into syrup as you will be starting with sap of a higher sugar content. Lift the layer of frozen ice, let the sap drain from it, and discard it. If the entire bucket is frozen, you can either wait until it completely thaws or until it partially thaws, pouring the liquid out and tossing the ice.

Storage: It is perfectly acceptable to mix and store sap from different types of maple trees. For the hobbyist at home, you will not notice a significant difference in the resulting syrup as a consequence of blending sap from different types of maple trees. The sap should be stored at a temperature of 38 degrees F or colder, used within 7 days of collection, and boiled prior to use to eliminate any possible bacteria growth. If there is still snow on the ground, you may keep the storage containers outside, placed in the shade, and packed with snow. You can also store the sap in your refrigerator or, for longer term storage, in your freezer. Remember that sap is like milk; it will spoil quickly if not kept cold. If your sap has taken on a yellow or milky color, or if it has an off smell, it has spoiled. Discard it (pouring it over a garden is a good idea) and start with a fresh batch.

Cleanliness and Sanitization

Cleanliness and Sanitization: Remember, you are making a food product so keeping your equipment and tools as clean as possible is very important. Bacteria love sugar and since maple sap has just enough, controlling bacterial growth is essential.

Cleanliness and sanitization of all equipment will have a direct impact on your results, including:

> **Quality of your maple syrup:** Bacteria present in the sap are killed in the boiling process but the byproduct will be a darker syrup. Syrup taste will also be impacted.

> **Sap flow:** Bacteria in the tap hole may cause the tree to start its natural healing process, either slowing or stopping the sap flow.

These tips are mentioned elsewhere in the book, but are worth repeating:

- Always clean your equipment at the beginning and end of every season, including buckets, spiles, and storage containers.

- Keep maple sap as cool as you can, 38 degrees Γ or colder. Store sap out of direct sunlight.

- Boil your sap as soon as possible, within 7 days of collection.

- Clean boiling equipment after each boil.

- Sterilize bottles or jars used to store your maple syrup.

Making Maple Syrup

As a rule of thumb, 10 gallons of sap can be boiled into 1 quart of syrup (a ratio of 40 to 1). The quantities will vary slightly due to the sugar content of the sap. Please note that boiling sap into syrup requires a lot of time and patience. This boiling project is best left to the outdoors unless you are no longer fond of your kitchen wallpaper as this task will surely take it off the walls! If you do decide to boil indoors, do so in small batches and ensure good ventilation. But, please consider yourself forewarned - the process will generate a lot of steam! If you choose to boil outdoors, make certain you are in compliance with any local regulations. FIRE SAFETY MUST BE YOUR HIGHEST PRIORITY, ESPECIALLY WHEN YOUNG CHILDREN ARE PRESENT.

Gather the necessary equipment and prepare to boil your maple sap into maple syrup:

- **Large Pot or Pan**: If boiling indoors (remember, only small batches), use the largest pot you would use on your stove. If boiling outdoors, a large pot or pan with a capacity of 3 – 6 gallons of sap is recommended. Wide, shallow pots / pans are preferred over deep ones as they allow more surface area for boiling. You may not want to use your best kitchen equipment, especially if boiling over an open fire since the exposed portion of the pot or pan may turn black. Stainless steel is recommended. Do not use any galvanized equipment to boil your sap as it is possible that lead could leach into the syrup. Boiling with multiple pots or pans will certainly expedite the process.

- **Smaller Pot**: When the sap is mostly boiled down, it can be transferred to a small pot to complete the boiling process indoors on the stove. A 2 or 3 quart pot can be used for this stage of the boiling process.

- **Heat Source:** Depending upon the amount of sap you have collected, you will most likely boil for several hours. There are a few options available as a heat source. Smaller batches can be boiled indoors on the stove. Another popular indoor option is to utilize a wood stove, placing the pot or pan on top of the stove. Outdoor options include a barbeque grill, an open fire pit, or even an outdoor fryer (like the ones used to deep fry a turkey). In the illustrated example (on following page), a shallow pit is dug, stones are used to support the walls, and metal bars are placed over the stones to provide support for the pot. Dry firewood, preferably split into small pieces, is required for this option. After you have a year or two of experience, you may choose to build or purchase a small evaporator. An evaporator will enable a more efficient boiling process but, for the hobbyist tapping just a few trees, the expense is relatively high. Through experience, you will develop a heat source that works best for your needs.

- **Sap:** Your collected sap will be required!

- **Candy Thermometer or Syrup Hydrometer:** As you near completion of the boil, a candy thermometer or maple syrup hydrometer is used to determine when your sap has turned into syrup. If you don't have either, a good approximation can be made by using the dip method (described later in this section).

- **Filter:** Once the syrup is produced, you will need to filter out any sediment. Large scale operations use wool or orlon filters but, for your small scale production, filter sheets can be purchased and cut to size. A coffee filter may also be used, but you will only be able to filter a small amount of syrup at a time. When using a coffee filter, you may need to force the syrup through the filter, often causing it to tear.

- **Bottle and Cap:** Sterile bottles and caps are used to store your finished maple syrup. You can reuse a glass bottle (sterilized in boiling water) from store bought syrup. Canning jars and lids may also be used. Be sure to use only food grade containers.

Now that you have gathered your supplies, you are ready to start boiling your maple syrup.

Heat Source: There are many options available as a heat source. In this example, an outdoor fire pit is used. A small pit is dug, using stones to

secure the walls of the pit. Metal bars are secured over the fire to support the pot. A fire is built in the pit with dried, split wood. As it will take several hours to boil your sap into syrup, a sufficient wood supply is required. **Fire safety must be your first priority, especially if young children are present.**

Boiling the Sap: Fill your large pot ¾ full with sap. Place the pot onto the heat source. Once the sap starts to boil down to ¼ - ½ the depth of

the pot, add more sap while maintaining the boil. Pre-heating some sap in a smaller pot will help maintain the boil. If the sap is foaming over the edge of the pot, a drop of vegetable oil or butter wiped onto the edge of the pot will help reduce this. You can also use a skimmer ladle and scoop the foam out of the pot.

Transfer to Smaller Pot: The boiling sap will take on a golden color. Once the sap has "mostly" boiled down, but still has a very fluid texture, it is time to transfer the sap into a smaller pot to finish the boil indoors. **The outdoor heat source should be fully extinguished at this point.**

Complete the Boiling: Once transferred to the smaller pot, the final boiling can be completed indoors. **It is important to watch the boiling sap very closely as it approaches syrup as it is more likely to boil over at this stage.** Continue to boil the sap until it takes on a consistency of syrup. There are several methods to determine if your sap has turned into syrup:

- <u>Maple Syrup Hydrometer and Hydrometer Test Cup:</u> The liquid is poured into the test cup and the hydrometer is lowered into the syrup. At this point, the hydrometer is read to determine if you have maple syrup. Follow the directions that are included with your hydrometer. Never drop the hydrometer into the test cup as this may cause the glass hydrometer to shatter.

- <u>Candy Thermometer:</u> Maple sap becomes syrup at a temperature of 7 degrees Fahrenheit above the boiling point of water. Note that the boiling point of water differs based on your elevation. When making smaller batches of syrup, 1 quart for example, a candy thermometer is preferred over a hydrometer and test cup.

- <u>Dip Method:</u> Dip a spoon into the sap/syrup. Syrup will stick to the spoon and "apron" as it runs off. Sap will run off the spoon as water would.

Filtering the Syrup: A small amount of sediment will be present in your syrup and should be filtered out using a food grade filter. Let the syrup cool slightly and then pour it through the filter, collecting it in a clean container. Filter sheets can be purchased and cut to size. A coffee filter can also be used, but you will only be able to filter a small amount of syrup at a time. When using a coffee filter, you often need to force the syrup through

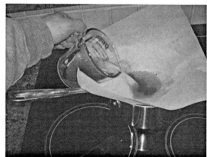

the filter, which can cause the filter to tear. If this happens, re-filter this portion of the syrup. Discard filters after use. Depending upon how much syrup is produced, you may need to use several filters.

You can also remove the sediment by allowing the syrup to stand over-night in the refrigerator. This allows the sediment to settle at the bottom and you can pour the "clean" syrup off into another container. The results will not be as good and you may waste a small amount of syrup using this process.

Bottle Your Syrup: Sterilize a bottle and cap (or multiple bottles and caps depending upon how much syrup you have produced) in boiling water. Bottle the maple syrup when it is hot (between 180 - 200 degrees F) to reduce the potential for spoilage. Using a funnel, pour the sediment free syrup into the bottle, cap, and refrigerate.

Your refrigerated syrup will last many months, largely dependent upon the level of sanitation and sterilization you observed during the collection, boiling, and bottling processes. Syrup can also be frozen (in a freezer safe container) to extend shelf life.

Enjoy your delicious maple syrup!

Other Uses for Maple Sap

Although the uses for maple sap are limited only by your imagination, this section of the guide suggests some common uses.

Treat sap like any other nutrient extracted from nature to be included in your diet. When you pick berries in a field, they can be eaten directly from the bush; however, it is generally a good idea to wash them first. Many drink sap straight from the collection bucket, but it is highly recommended to boil your sap prior to any use to kill bacteria that may be present. To effectively kill bacteria, bring the sap to a rolling boil and then let it boil one additional minute.

Drink Your Sap: Native Indians and loggers have a long history of drinking maple sap. Iroquois Indians drank the spring sap as a way to cleanse the body. In South Korea, drinking maple sap is a spring ritual and is believed to be good for the bones and provide other health benefits. Drinking maple sap is also popular in China and Japan while Birch sap is popular in Russia. There is a belief that sap contains many nutrients, including iron, that are drained from the body over a long winter. Drinking sap can be a source of revitalization. Keep a jug of maple sap in the refrigerator and enjoy it on a spring day.

Coffee and Tea: When making your coffee or tea, use sap instead of water to provide a naturally sweetened flavor.

Cooking: Virtually all recipes that call for water can use sap as a substitute, providing a slightly sweeter outcome. For example, use sap when boiling rice, cooking pasta, and making soup or pancakes.

Brewing Beer: If you brew your own beer, use sap instead of water to generate a sweet, maple flavor.

Garden: When the sap starts to flow, you may collect more than you can use. If this is the case, pour the excess sap (or even spoiled sap) into your garden to put nature's resources back into the earth. Your garden vegetables can then draw upon these nutrients.

Birds: Share your excess sap with Mother Nature's creatures. Freeze your sap, thaw it in late spring, and fill your birdbath or hummingbird feeder with it.

End of Season

All good things come to an end and the flow of sap is no exception. Once the temperature consistently remains above freezing and buds begin to swell on your maple trees, it is time to stop collecting. A yellow or milky sap in your bucket also highlights the end of the maple sugaring season. At this point, remove the taps, clean your equipment, and store them for next year.

Removing the Taps: With a pair of pliers, firmly grab hold of the tap and pull it out of the tree. Do not plug the hole. The maple tree will naturally grow over the tap hole.

Cleaning Equipment: Prior to storage, it is essential to clean all your equipment. Making a mixture of one part unscented household bleach (such as Clorox® Regular-Bleach) to 20 parts clean water, use a brush or cloth to scrub your equipment. Triple rinse with hot water and dry thoroughly.

Storage: Store your supplies in a dry location, free from dust.

Frequently Asked Questions

Does tapping hurt the tree?

Tapping a tree does create a wound, but it does not endanger the health

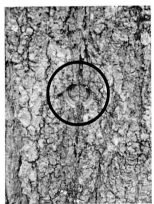

of a tree if the proper tapping guidelines are followed. The tap hole is a wound but one that a healthy tree can readily recover from. Commercial syrup producers are able to tap trees for decades without adversely affecting the health of the tree. A vigorous tree will heal, or grow over, a tap hole in one year. It may take less healthy trees up to 3 years to grow over a tap hole. Pictured is an example of a tap hole after one year of recovery.

What is the sugar content of my sap?

Sugar content depends upon many variables, including the type of tree, weather conditions, previous summer's growing season, soil type, tree genetics, and when during the flow of the season the sap is collected. The sugar content in the sap of a Sugar Maple tree can fluctuate between 1.5% and 2.5%.

How much sap does it take to make maple syrup?

The general rule of thumb for maple sap is that it takes 40 parts sap to produce 1 part syrup, but this is dependent upon the sugar content. This translates into 40 gallons of sap to produce 1 gallon of syrup (or 10 gallons of sap for one quart of syrup).

How much sap will each tap produce in a season?

This is dependent upon many factors, but you can generally expect to collect 5 - 15 gallons of sap per tap.

What makes sap flow?

Sap flow is caused by pressure difference within the tree when the temperature fluctuates. Nighttime temperatures below freezing and daytime temperatures above freezing create pressure conditions ideal for sap flow.

Other than maple, what types of trees can be tapped?

While this guide focuses on maple trees, other types of trees can be tapped. For example, Birch and Walnut trees can be tapped and will yield a sweet sap. These trees are not generally used in commercial production of syrup because the sugar content is lower. Alaska, where maple trees do not grow, has a thriving birch sap industry.

What are the different grades of maple syrup?

Each region has its own grading guidelines. Within the U.S., there are slight variances in grading standards; however, between the U.S. and Canada, the grades are substantially different. The U.S. grading system adheres to the following grades:

Grade A Light Amber: A light amber color, with a light and mild maple flavor.

Grade A Medium Amber: A medium amber color, with a bit more maple flavor. This is the most popular grade for table use.

Grade A Dark Amber: A dark amber color, with a strong maple flavor.

Grade B: Dark in color, generally used for cooking and baking.

It is interesting to note that the grades correspond to the point in the season during which the sap was collected. Grade A Light Amber generally utilizes sap from the earliest point in the season and Grade B generally from the latest point in the season.

Note that at the time of writing this book, there is a proposal to standardize on a universal grading system that will be used by all of North America. The proposed new grading system:

Golden Maple Syrup with color not less than 75% Tc (Light Transmittance) and a Delicate Taste: Pure maple syrup in this class has a light to more pronounced golden color and a delicate or mild taste. It is the product of choice for consumers preferring a lighter colored maple syrup with a delicate or mild taste.

Amber Maple Syrup with color less than 75% Tc but not less than 50% Tc and a Rich Taste: Pure maple syrup in this class has a light amber color and a rich or full-bodied taste. It is the product of choice for consumers preferring a full-body tasting syrup of medium taste intensity.

Dark Maple Syrup with color less than 50% Tc but not less than 25% Tc and a Robust Taste: Pure maple syrup in this class has a dark color and a more robust or stronger taste than syrup in lighter color classes. It is the product of choice for consumers preferring a dark colored syrup with substantial or robust taste.

Very Dark Maple Syrup with color less than 25% Tc and a Strong Taste: Pure maple syrup in this class has a very strong taste. It is generally recommended for cooking purposes but some consumers may prefer it for table use.

What is the difference between maple sap and maple syrup?

Maple sap is a clear, water-like liquid captured when a maple tree is tapped. Maple syrup is produced by boiling sap, concentrating it into a sweet syrup.

Who first discovered the process of making maple syrup?

It is well documented that native Indians in the United States and Canada were the first producers of maple products. Native Indians were more likely to either drink the sap or make maple sugar products as storing the liquid syrup would have been difficult. Early European settlers learned maple sap collection and processing skills from these native Indians. And, of course, over the years, the process of collecting and processing sap has been refined.

How big should a maple tree be before tapping it?

A maple tree should be at least 12 inches in diameter before tapping it. Larger trees can support multiple taps. For example, trees 21-27 inches in diameter can support 2 taps and trees greater than 27 inches in diameter can support 3 taps.

At the end of the maple sugaring season, after removing spiles, should the tap hole be plugged?

No, do not attempt to plug the tap hole. The tree will naturally heal the hole, and plugging the hole with a foreign material will disrupt the natural healing process.

Maple Sugaring at Home

Resources

If you are interested in learning more about maple sap or maple syrup production, there are many resources available to you.

Library: Your local library likely has numerous books on maple trees, sap collection, and the production of maple syrup. In addition to this guide, there are several well written books to assist the maple sugaring hobbyist. These include:

> **Backyard Sugarin': A Complete How-To Guide**, by Rink Mann. In addition to providing basic information on maple sugaring, this book provides detailed information as to how to build a backyard evaporator.

> **Making Maple Syrup the Old Fashioned Way**, by Noel Perrin. This short publication details three systems for maple sugaring, from the backyard hobbyist to the commercial operation.

> **The Illustrated Book of Trees**, by William Carey Grimm. This book will help you identify your maple trees.

> **North American Maple Syrup Producers Manual**, Produced by Ohio State University Extension, in Cooperation with The North American Maple Syrup Council. The most extensive guide to everything maple syrup.

Internet: Visit **www.TapMyTrees.com** for more information on maple sugaring at home and to purchase any supplies you may need. The Tap My Trees Facebook page (www.facebook.com/tapmytrees) provides invaluable feedback on experiences from the community of maple sugaring hobbyists. The Cornell Sugar Maple Research and Extension Program, found at http://maple.dnr.cornell.edu, provides excellent information to both the hobbyist and experienced. You can also utilize Yahoo, Google, or Bing searches to find extensive content on all aspects of maple sap collection and maple syrup production.

Local Maple Syrup Producers: If you live in an area where maple trees grow, there is almost certainly a local producer of maple syrup. This will often be a family-owned business. When the sap is flowing, local producers often provide tours of their operation or hold informational sessions about the production of maple syrup.

You: After reading this guide , tapping your trees, and making maple syrup, you are an experienced hobbyist. Spread the word about this fun activity and help your friends get started!

Quick Reference Checklist

Here is a quick checklist of maple sugaring supplies.

SAP COLLECTION

- ☐ Maple Tree
- ☐ Drill with 7/16 drill bit
- ☐ Spile/Hook
- ☐ Bucket
- ☐ Lid
- ☐ Cheesecloth
- ☐ Hammer
- ☐ Pliers

SAP STORAGE

- ☐ Food Grade Containers

MAKING SYRUP

- ☐ Maple Sap
- ☐ Heat Source
- ☐ Pot (large and small)
- ☐ Filter
- ☐ Candy Thermometer (optional)
- ☐ Hydrometer (optional)
- ☐ Hydrometer Test Cup (optional)
- ☐ Finished product container (jar and lid)

Notes

Use the following pages to note anything from mapping your yard to recording your personal maple sugaring experiences and triumphs!

Notes

Notes

Notes